The Bee's Sneeze

'The Bee's Sneeze'
An original concept by Kate Poels
© Kate Poels 2025

Illustrated by Letizia Rizzo

Published by MAVERICK ARTS PUBLISHING LTD
Suite 1, Hillreed House, 54 Queen Street,
Horsham, West Sussex, RH13 5AD
© Maverick Arts Publishing Limited April 2025
+44 (0)1403 256941

ISBN 978-1-83511-054-6

Printed in India

Maverick
publishing
www.maverickbooks.co.uk

Turquoise

This book is rated as: Turquoise Band (Guided Reading)

The Bee's Sneeze

By Kate Poels

Illustrated by
Letizia Rizzo

Ned was a bee.

Most bees like to fly and dance and buzz between the flowers, but not Ned.

Ned's wings got tired when he did too much flying.

And his legs tangled when he tried to dance.

But worst of all were the flowers, because they made him sneeze.

Ned was a bee who was much happier just bumbling around.

The other bees teased him.

"Come on Ned," they said.

"Why won't you join us?"

But Ned always said, "No."

One day, there was a big competition called the Great Flying Bee.

All the bees from miles around came to see who were the best fliers.

Ned made a picnic and went to watch

with his good friend Fi Bee.

"Will you enter any of the races?" Fi asked.

"No," said Ned. "I am going to watch while

I eat my sandwiches."

"I am going to try to win the crown for the

fastest flier," said Fi. "I've been practising."

Fi had to wait because the competition to see which bee could fly the highest was about to start. Ned cheered when they took off. He looked up into the sky to see how far they went.

The winner was a bee called Maggie.

She had flown up past the clouds and tickled

the tummy of an aeroplane.

Queen Bee gave her a gold medal.

The trick fliers were next. They had to fly through hoops, weave around poles and whizz through tunnels.

"That looks very tricky," said Fi.

"It looks very tiring," said Ned.

All of the trick fliers were really good,

but Ravi Bee was the best of all.

He won the gold rosette.

Then it was Fi Bee's turn as the

speed fliers lined up for their race.

"Good luck," said Ned. "Have fun."

Fi came in second place and was given

a silver medal. Ned clapped loudly when

Queen Bee hung it around Fi's neck.

A trumpet played and Ned turned around to see what was happening.

Ned got ready too. He stood up and went to find a good spot to watch from. Fi Bee came to join him.

"Did you see me fly?" she asked.

"Yes," said Ned. "You were brilliant."

As the first bees began to fly,

Ned felt a tickle in his nose.

He looked at Fi and saw the big bunch of

flowers she was holding. "Oh no!" he said.

The tickle got bigger and bigger until it burst out of him with a loud ACHOOOO! It was the biggest sneeze any bee had ever known.

It shot Ned backwards into the arena.

The sneeze was so big that it made him

twist and spin as he went.

He looped the loop and turned

three spirals before landing in

the middle of the arena.

All the other bees went wild.

"Ned," they shouted. "You are the greatest freestyle flier ever!"

"Me?" Ned asked.

"Yes!" they cheered.

"Hooray for Ned!"

"Here is your prize," said Queen Bee.

"The Great Flying Bee gold cup and a

lovely big bunch of..."

"No!" said Ned. "Not flowers—ah, ah, ah,

ACHOOOO!"

Ned left the flowers behind, but he was very pleased to take the gold cup home.

He placed it carefully on a shelf.

Ned was very proud to be the greatest freestyle flier. But Ned was still a bee who liked to keep his feet on the ground. And he was also a bee who kept well away from flowers.

29

Quiz

1. "Bees like to fly and dance and _____
between the flowers, but not Ned."
a) sing
b) buzz
c) crash

2. What is the big competition called?
a) Grand Buzz Bee
b) Best Flier Triers
c) Great Flying Bee

3. What contest does Fi Bee enter?
a) Fastest Flier
b) Speedy Flybee
c) Highest Flier

4. Who won the gold rosette?

a) Ravi Bee

b) Maggie

c) Fi Bee

5. What is Ned's favourite contest?

a) Trick flying

b) The freestyle

c) Speed flying

Book Bands for Guided Reading

Pink
Red
Yellow
Blue
Green
Orange
Turquoise
Purple
Gold
White

The Institute of Education book banding system is a scale of colours that reflects the various levels of reading difficulty. The bands are assigned by taking into account the content, the language style, the layout and phonics. Word, phrase and sentence level work is also taken into consideration.

Maverick Early Readers are a bright, attractive range of books covering the pink to white bands. All of these books have been book banded for guided reading to the industry standard and edited by a leading educational consultant.

To view the whole Maverick Readers scheme, visit our website at www.maverickearlyreaders.com

Or scan the QR code above to view our scheme instantly!